Table of Contents

MW00700743

Capitalization and End Punctuation

Lesson 1

Remember to use capital letters and end punctuation.

Capitalize:
- the first word in every sentence.
- the names of people and pets.
- the word I.
- the names of relatives such as Mother and Father when they are used as a name or with another name. (When will Mother come home? Did Uncle Jim call?)
- names of days, months, holidays, places, and nationalities.
- titles of respect such as Doctor, Judge, and Miss.
- abbreviated titles of respect such as Mr., Mrs., or Dr.
- initials that stand for a person's name such as J. F. Kennedy.

Draw a circle around the first letter of each word that should begin with a capital letter. Put a period, question mark, or exclamation point at the end of each sentence.

1. shirley made two new friends on saturday

2. the children's favorite teacher is ms alberts

3. did dr. swift give you a penicillin shot

4. how exciting

5. do you remember when neil armstrong walked on the moon

6. jackie and i took a train to new york on may 18, 1980

7. will father and mr. jackson be on the same bowling team

8. did you see pepper chase that brown cat up the tree

9. our team won

10. we watched the parade on new year's day

11. my uncle's friend, judge w. heinz, is german

12. having chicken pox can be very annoying

13. what fun

14. professor jenkins left a stack of books on the desk

15. cousin billie and i ate chinese noodles at j.j.'s house

Punctuation

Lesson 2

You're on your way!

- Put a period after abbreviations such as Mrs., Dr., Ave., and CA.
- Put a period after an initial such as Carla R. Foster.
- Put a comma after each part of an address.
- In a date, put a comma after the day and after the year if words follow it in a sentence.
- Use commas to separate three or more items in a series.
- Use a comma after words such as **oh, well, yes,** and **no** when they are the first word in a sentence.
- Use a comma(s) to set off the name of a person being spoken to.
- Use an apostrophe wherever letters are left out in a contraction.
- Use an apostrophe after a noun to show ownership. (The man's hat)

Put in the correct punctuation marks.

1. Larry did you see the batter hit the ball over the fence?

2. Barbara Bertha and Betty are sisters.

3. Mr R B Draper wasnt elected mayor in the June 10 1998 election.

4. Karen were you in San Francisco CA last week?

5. Why did you throw Monicas toys in the pool Mike?

6. Do you like comedy mystery or adventure movies the best?

7. That batters bat broke into two pieces.

8. Yes I did go camping on August 14 1998.

9. B J hasnt finished her homework yet.

10. Prof Diaz have you met Dr Petrozelli?

11. Jimmy piled lettuce tomatoes and onions on his hamburger.

12. When Mary do you expect to finish your chores?

13. Ms Kent moved to Wilton Minnesota on Saturday.

14. Well Im not sure that we are going to Norway Iowa next year.

15. Tammy please buy a loaf of bread a bottle of milk and one dozen eggs.

Quotation Marks

Lesson 3

Is it a direct quotation or an indirect quotation?

Put quotation marks before and after a direct quotation.
Direct quotations are the speaker's exact words.

> "Come over soon," said Jacob.
> Jacob said, "Come over soon."
> Jacob asked, "When are you coming over?"

Do not use quotation marks in an indirect quotation.
Indirect quotations tell what the speaker said without using the speaker's direct words.

> Jacob asked us to come over soon.

Write **D.Q.** before each sentence that is a direct quotation.
Put quotation marks before and after each direct quotation.
Write **I.Q.** before each sentence that is an indirect quotation.

1. _____ May Tony and I go to the fair, asked Nancy.

2. _____ Andy told me about his trip to Canada.

3. _____ The teacher said that we should read chapter three before we answer the questions.

4. _____ Meet me in the park, Dan, said Ricky.

5. _____ Jonathan asked Mother to buy him a new jacket.

6. _____ Bobby asked, Will Uncle Fred come tomorrow?

7. _____ Kenny asked if we had seen Jerry today.

8. _____ The bus driver told us to watch the steps.

9. _____ Yolanda wanted to know about our first day at camp.

10. _____ The canary flew out of the cage! shouted Terry.

11. _____ Do you know how to ice skate? asked Paul.

12. _____ Annie asked, Dad, may I borrow your hammer and saw?

13. _____ Mrs. Greyson asked me to be at her house in one hour.

Literary Titles

Lesson 4

It gets heavy but it's worth the effort!

Name _____

Date _____

Capitalize the first, last, and important words in the titles of books, stories, poems, and songs.

Do not capitalize words such as **a, an, and, at, by, for, in, of, the,** and **with**, unless they are the first word in the title.

> **O**ver the **R**ainbow

Underline the title of a book when it is used in a sentence.
Put quotation marks around the title of a song, poem, or story when it is used in a sentence.

> Have you read <u>A Free Nation</u> yet?

> Jill sang "Home on the Range" for her parents.

Draw a circle around the first letter of each word that should begin with a capital letter. Use quotation marks and underlining in the right places.

1. Penny played carry me back to old virginny on the piano.

2. jingle bells is a Christmas song.

3. Liz called her report the start of the monsoon.

4. Tara read the book the victory at ribbon pass.

5. Sara Shope wrote the story learning to fish.

6. Gary reported on the book a famous race horse.

7. red badge of courage is a great book.

8. mice is a poem written by Rose Flyeman.

9. race against the clock is a story about a girl named Sarah.

10. Irving Berlin's first hit song was alexander's ragtime band.

11. Jack London wrote the call of the wild.

12. she'll be comin' 'round the mountain is a silly song.

13. The musician Jean Sibelius wrote valse triste.

14. Barry bought the book a scout's handbook.

Sentences

Lesson 5

Write good sentences.

Sentences are groups of words that tell or ask us something.

Sue is going to babysit the Alan children.

Fragments are groups of words that do not tell or ask something.

the Alan children

Run-ons are usually made when end punctuation is left out of sentences.

Wrong:
Sue is going to babysit the Alan children, she likes them.

Right:
Sue is going to babysit the Alan children. She likes them.

Change the following groups of words into good sentences. Use capital letters and punctuation.

1. a popular story: _____

2. only five minutes: _____

3. my favorite dessert is cake, i like chocolate: _____

   _____

4. the chores are done now i can swim: _____

   _____

5. we used all the paper we will need more: _____

   _____

6. hitting the wall: _____

7. val has two blue sweaters they are like mine: _____

   _____

8. the final score: _____

9. windy day: _____

10. milk and orange juice: _____

Word Usage

Lesson 6

It's as easy as falling off a log!

Write a sentence for each word. Use capital letters and punctuation in the right places.

1. himself: _____
2. herself: _____
3. themselves: _____
4. may: _____
5. can: _____
6. sit: _____
7. set: _____
8. let: _____
9. leave: _____
10. good: _____
11. well: _____
12. they're: _____
13. there: _____
14. their: _____
15. off: _____
16. of: _____
17. must have: _____
18. to: _____
19. two: _____
20. too: _____
21. never: _____
22. nothing: _____
23. no one: _____
24. nowhere: _____

Contractions

Lesson 7

Contractions are two words combined with a letter or letters left out.

Use an **apostrophe** to show where the letters were left out.

is not = isn't	will not = won't
what is = what's	they will = they'll
we have = we've	you are = you're

Keep moving! You're doing GREAT!

Write a contraction for each pair of words.

1. it is _____

2. I am _____

3. that is _____

4. we are _____

5. what is _____

6. we have _____

7. he is _____

8. you have _____

9. you are _____

10. do not _____

11. it will _____

12. will not _____

13. had not _____

14. have not _____

15. they will _____

16. where is _____

17. should not _____

18. we will _____

19. were not _____

20. are not _____

21. I have _____

22. you will _____

23. let us _____

24. can not _____

25. he will _____

26. did not _____

27. she will _____

28. does not _____

29. they have _____

30. they are _____

31. she is _____

32. has not _____

33. there is _____

34. is not _____

35. I will _____

36. who is _____

37. was not _____

38. would not _____

Nouns

Lesson 8

Does it name a person, place, or thing?

A **noun** is a word that names a person, place, or thing (girl, zoo, book).
Draw a line under each noun.

1. Henry and Jess live in a small town.

2. The mouse is a rodent.

3. Joey shined his shoes before going to school.

4. Math is my favorite subject.

5. Bertha and Tim scrubbed the floors and washed the windows.

6. Does your favorite meal consist of hamburgers and fried potatoes?

7. Grandpa parked his car in our neighbor's driveway.

8. Ellen brushes her long hair.

9. My father works for the city.

10. Neither Barbara nor Connie plays the piano very well.

11. Mother paid twenty dollars for the new blouse.

12. Rose sent Grandma a bouquet of daisies for her birthday.

13. Otto won the first four races!

14. John and Marta tied the newspapers into five large bundles.

15. Did Kisha see the Statue of Liberty?

16. Carol must work in Las Vegas this weekend.

17. Michelle and Jonathan are moving to a new house on Bogardus Avenue.

18. The children on the school bus were making loud noises.

19. Did Jess break the crate of apples?

20. Many farmers grow grapes in the Coachella Valley.

Common and Proper Nouns

Lesson 9

Name _____

Date _____

Don't let it bog you down!

A **common noun** is a word that names **any** person, place, or thing. Words like river, country, and boy are common nouns. Common nouns do not begin with a capital letter unless they are the first word in a sentence.

A **proper noun** is a word that names a **special** person, place, or thing. Ohio River, Mexico, and Danny are proper nouns. Proper nouns always begin with a capital letter.

Circle each common noun.

Draw a line under each proper noun.

1. Have you heard of a game called badminton?

2. Badminton is a very popular game in some parts of the world.

3. Badminton is the national game in countries such as Thailand, Indonesia, and Malaysia.

4. Many people in the European countries of England, Denmark, and Sweden also enjoy the game.

5. A man named Rudy Hortono, from Indonesia, won the badminton championship eight times.

6. Mr. Hortono has streets, statues, and even babies named after him.

7. Chris Kinard has been the United States' badminton champion five times.

8. He has received a badminton scholarship to U.C.L.A. and free trips to countries such as England and Canada.

9. Badminton is an indoor sport.

10. Using long wooden rackets, the players hit shuttlecocks or birds over a five-foot-high net.

11. Badminton is like tennis in some ways.

12. A good player must move quickly and be able to hit well.

13. At first the players in the United States received only trophies.

14. Since 1978, they can play against other players for prize money.

15. Badminton players in the United States hope that the game will become as popular as tennis.

Singular and Plural Nouns

Lesson 10

Hang in there!

Name _____

Date _____

A **singular noun** names one person. place, or thing.
A **plural noun** names more than one person, place, or thing.

To change most singular nouns to plural nouns, add **s** (cup - cups).
To nouns ending in **sh, ch, s, x,** add **es** (lunch - lunches).
To nouns ending in **y** after a vowel, add **s** (key - keys).
To nouns ending in **y** after a consonant, change the **y** to **i** and add **es** (fly - flies).
To nouns ending in **o** after a vowel, add **s** (rodeo - rodeos).
To nouns ending in **o** after a consonant, add **es** (tomato - tomatoes). Words that
    refer to music are exceptions (piano - pianos).
To nouns ending in **f** or **fe**, change the **f** or **fe** to **ves**
    (calf - calves or knife - knives).
Some nouns completely change their spelling (mouse - mice).

Change these singular nouns to plural nouns.

1. candy _____

2. knife _____

3. piano _____

4. ax _____

5. potato _____

6. army _____

7. copy _____

8. tooth _____

9. hero _____

10. half _____

11. friend _____

12. child _____

13. journey _____

14. solo _____

15. calf _____

16. shelf _____

17. duty _____

18. grocery _____

19. enemy _____

20. city _____

21. cupful _____

22. loaf _____

23. baby _____

24. foot _____

25. valley _____

26. tax _____

27. tomato _____

28. life _____

Possessive Nouns

Lesson 11

Name _____

Date _____

To make a singular noun show possession or ownership, add an **apostrophe** and an **s** (bird - bird**'s**).

To make a plural noun show possession or ownership, add an **apostrophe** after the final **s** (girls - girls').

If the plural noun does not end in **s**, add an **apostrophe** and an **s** as you would for a singular noun (children - children's).

Put apostrophes in the right places.

1. The strong wind caused the spiders web to fall apart.

2. Mothers garden is filled with juicy melons.

3. Our two dogs dinners were turned over by the frightened cat.

4. The childrens bicycles are parked out front.

5. Fluffys green eyes glowed in the moonlight.

6. Eddie washed Mr. Samuels car.

7. The calves mother took a rest.

8. A taco is my sisters favorite treat.

9. That dogs muddy paws left a trail on Mothers clean floor.

Write the correct word.

10. Ladies hats are now on sale.

11. The girls softball team beat the boys softball team.

12. Karens dress has puffy sleeves and a bow tie.

13. That boys skateboard was stolen.

14. Uncle Jims house has a computer room.

15. Todays newspaper never arrived.

16. Was Americas first president George Washington?

17. That bees buzzing frightened Jennys little sister.

18. Mikes birthday cakes icing melted in the hot sun.

Review Test 1
Lesson 12

Name _____

Date _____

Circle the first letter of each word that should begin with a capital letter.
Put punctuation marks in the right places.

1. donnas dog, skipper, ran across meyer ave to palm park

3. have you seen mother and aunt vivian

3. look out

4. my parents and i visited dr bensons office on may 2 1998.

5. did mr g daniels arrive in phoenix arizona on tuesday

6. gail jerry and i walked to the shore

7. kelly please wait for me

8. the irish celebrate st patricks day every year

Use quotation marks and underlining in the right places. Circle the first letter of each word that should begin with a capital letter.

9. i have invited eight friends to my party, said aaron.

10. each student wrote a story using the title my favorite day of the year.

11. Henry read the book a sea otter in my backyard.

Write the contractions.

12. should not_____

13. he will_____

14. they are _____

15. that is _____

Circle each common noun. Draw a line under each proper noun.

16. Benny and his friend walked to the Westwood Theater to see a movie.

Change each singular noun to its plural form.

17. mouse _____

18. tax_____

19. tray_____

20. wharf_____

21. piano _____

22. radio _____

23. berry _____

24. potato _____

Pronouns

Lesson 13

Don't give up! You're doing great!

Name _____

Date _____

A **noun** is a word that names a person, place, or thing.

A **pronoun** is a word that takes the place of a noun.
The most common pronouns are: **I, my, mine, me, he, his, him, she, her, hers, it, its, we, our, ours, us, you, your, yours, they, their, theirs,** and **them.**

Fill in each blank with a **pronoun.**

1. " _____ wish I lived in Vermont," said Nan.

2. "Why do _____ want to live in Vermont?" asked

   _____ mother.

3. " _____ snows in Vermont," _____ answered.

4. "All it does is rain in _____ town," _____ said.

5. "Would _____ like to pretend that _____ have snow?"
   asked Mother.

6. "How can _____ do that?" asked Nan.

7. "First ask Mr. Granger if _____ can borrow _____
   popcorn popper," said Mother.

8. "What will _____ do with the popper?" Nan asked.

9. " _____ will make something out of the popcorn," replied Mother.

10. After Nan made the popcorn, _____ put butter on

    _____ hands.

11. Meanwhile, _____ mother poured syrup over the popcorn.

12. Together, _____ rolled the popcorn into three balls.

13. "Can _____ tell what _____ are going to do with the
    popcorn?" asked Mother.

14. " _____ am going to make a popcorn snowman!"
    Nan exclaimed.

15. Nan really enjoyed _____ popcorn snowman.

Nouns and Pronouns

Lesson 14

A noun is a word that names a person, place, or thing.

A pronoun is a word that takes the place of a noun.

Tell whether each word is a **noun** or a **pronoun**.

You're getting the "drift" of it!

1. friend _____
2. David _____
3. I _____
4. my _____
5. California _____
6. their _____
7. school _____
8. her _____
9. me _____
10. churches _____
11. people _____
12. they _____
13. yours _____
14. him _____
15. Crooked Creek _____
16. game _____
17. us _____
18. Dr. Larson _____
19. you _____
20. we _____
21. language _____
22. boy _____
23. it _____

24. them _____
25. building _____
26. theirs _____
27. our _____
28. mother _____
29. pony _____
30. mine _____
31. hospital _____
32. wagon _____
33. he _____
34. his _____
35. upstairs _____
36. neighbor _____
37. machine _____
38. she _____
39. Idaho _____
40. your _____
41. Michelle _____
42. ours _____
43. its _____
44. hers _____
45. telephone _____
46. England _____

Verbs

Lesson 15

I am going to read these rules again!

Name _____

Date _____

A **verb** is a word that shows action. Some verbs are used alone.

(She **walked** home.)

Sometimes a sentence needs more than one verb to make the statement clear. These words are called **helping verbs**.

(She **had walked** home with me.)

Some common helping verbs are: **am, are, is, was, were, do, did, have, has, had, can,** and **may.**

Some verbs help show the appearance or condition of something. These verbs are called **linking verbs**.

(The food **was** delicious.)

Some common linking verbs are: **am, is, are, was, were, be, being, been, seem, become, appear, remain, look,** and **feel.**

Tell whether the word in bold is a **verb, linking verb,** or **helping verb.**

1. _____ Corrine **is** a good student.

2. _____ Jacob **is** leaving for school.

3. _____ They **are** my best friends.

4. _____ Sammy and I **played** soccer all afternoon.

5. _____ The tiny baby **ate** all its breakfast.

6. _____ I **feel** wonderful!

7. _____ My family and I **traveled** to Canada last year.

8. _____ "I **am** cooking dinner now," said Mother.

9. _____ She **became** the best long-distance runner.

10. _____ The boys **hit** the ball over the wall two times.

11. _____ Nancy and Francine **looked** lovely.

12. _____ I **played** badminton several times.

13. _____ The strong wind **blew** all the corn stalks down.

14. _____ They **are** a great family.

15. _____ The sixth grade team **is** winning the game.

16. _____ We **have** been to the seashore.

Verb Phrases
Lesson 16

Name _____

Date _____

A **verb phrase** contains one or more helping verbs along with the main verb.

Terry **had drawn** a beautiful picture.

William **must have worn** an overcoat.

Were the children **walking** to school?

Draw a line under the **verb phrase** in each sentence.

1. The books had fallen from the shelf.
2. We have eaten our dinner.
3. Were you swimming today?
4. Did Ellen see the circus parade?
5. I should have done all my homework.
6. The directions were written on the chalkboard.

That's it! You're going to get it!

Use each verb phrase in a short sentence.

7. have been: _____
8. were driven: _____
9. was seen: _____
10. has read: _____
11. could have done: _____
12. had been called: _____
13. was walking: _____
14. had thrown: _____
15. is cooking: _____
16. did close: _____
17. had forgotten: _____
18. should have gone: _____

Subjects and Predicates

Lesson 17

Name _____

Date _____

Every sentence has two parts: the **subject** and the **predicate.**
The subject is what or who is being talked about.
The predicate tells what the subject is doing or did.

My friend, Glenda, babysits every Saturday.

Complete Subject: My friend, Glenda,
Complete Predicate: babysits every Saturday.

Draw one line under the complete subject.
Draw two lines under the complete predicate.

1. Sandra ran to the post office.

2. Many monkeys live in trees.

3. Paul emptied the container of milk.

4. My father drove to San Francisco in just one day.

5. The rain fell gently against my bedroom window.

6. My cousins attend a private school.

7. Six inches of snow covered the ground.

8. We watched the fireworks from our front yard.

9. The small child coughed all night.

10. Aunt Susan wrote me a long letter.

11. The little boy with curly hair is my brother.

12. The driver of the small red car stopped by Pat's house.

13. Mother soaked her tired feet in warm water.

14. The sleepy children dressed for school.

15. The large dog with the brown spots jumps the fence each day.

16. Our tiny canary flew out of its cage.

17. David rides the bus to school.

18. The loud noise awakened the Jessup children.

Direct Objects

Lesson 18

A **direct object** is a noun or pronoun that answers the question **"What?"** or **"Whom?"** after the verb.

Andy watched the **parade.**

What did Andy watch? He watched the parade. Parade is the direct object in this sentence.

Jeff took **Kelly** to the library.

Jeff took whom to the library? He took Kelly to the library. Kelly is the direct object in this sentence.

Circle the **direct object** in each sentence.

1. Patricia has completed her book report.

2. Georgia baked a cheesecake this morning.

3. The water balloon hit Jack in the face.

4. The children gave Mother a surprise.

5. Ida hit a home run.

6. Mrs. Bennett searched her purse.

7. That customer received his package two days late.

8. Mr. and Mrs. Moorman took their children to the beach.

9. Vicky and I admired Shelly's new blouse.

10. Carrie watched the children in the park.

11. Aunt Greta served apple pie for dessert.

12. Mom took me shopping.

13. The librarian checked all the books.

14. We had cheese sandwiches.

15. Mike joined Edna at the park.

16. Mr. Lucas spotted his truck.

17. Grandma held Maryann in her arms.

18. Skippy drank all his water.

You're doing a great job!

Indirect Objects
Lesson

An **indirect object** is a word that tells **"to whom"** or **"for whom"** something is done. An indirect object usually comes between the verb and the direct object.

Mother made **Sarah** a new dress.

For whom did Mother make a new dress? She made it for Sarah. Sarah is the indirect object in this sentence.

What is the direct object of the sample sentence? What did Mother make? Dress is the direct object.

Circle the **indirect object** in each sentence. The direct object is in heavy type.

1. Larry gave everyone a piece of **paper**.

2. Uncle George sent Nicholas an autographed **baseball**.

3. The children wouldn't show me their **puppy**.

4. Lucy told her friends a **secret**.

5. Mrs. Tagawa made us some **rice cakes**.

6. Mom left Dad a **note**.

That's the trick!

7. The class gave Miss McGregor the **flowers**.

8. Grandma and Grandpa bought Maria a **bicycle** for her birthday.

9. Mother served Mrs. Lawson **tea** and **cookies**.

10. Betty passed Shirley the box of **pencils**.

11. Ginger played her relatives a **tune** on the piano.

12. I told Amy a bedtime **story**.

13. Yolanda handed Ralph the **platter**.

14. Aunt Annie and Uncle Minton gave the boys a big **hug**.

15. Joey and Teddy sent Grandma Olga a pretty **card**.

16. Mary and Chet gave us the **details**.

17. Sophie brought Mom fresh **fish**.

18. Aunt Sophie and Uncle Moxie sent their nephews two **hats**.

20   FS123255 Skill Drill Grammar Grade 4–5

Synonyms and Antonyms
Lesson 20

A **synonym** is a word that means **nearly the same** as another word.
A few synonyms for the word **great** are big, wide, and large.

An **antonym** is a word that means the **opposite** of another word.
A few antonyms for the word **great** are little, narrow, and small.

Write three **synonyms** for each word.

1. pretty: _____ _____ _____

2. hot: _____ _____ _____

3. old: _____ _____ _____

4. early: _____ _____ _____

5. light: _____ _____ _____

6. remove: _____ _____ _____

7. tame: _____ _____ _____

8. large: _____ _____ _____

9. quick: _____ _____ _____

Write three **antonyms** for each word.

10. pretty: _____ _____ _____

11. hot: _____ _____ _____

12. old: _____ _____ _____

13. early: _____ _____ _____

14. light: _____ _____ _____

15. remove: _____ _____ _____

16. tame: _____ _____ _____

17. large _____ _____ _____

18. quick: _____ _____ _____

Word Usage: a and an

Lesson 21

The word **a** is used before a word that begins with a consonant sound.

   Danny painted **a picture** of his friends.

The word **an** is used before a word that begins with a vowel sound.

   Patty put **an apple** in her lunch sack.

Hurray for you!

Write **a** or **an** in each blank.

1. _____ family	2. _____ ocean	3. _____ hiker
4. _____ ship	5. _____ person	6. _____ flower
7. _____ hotel	8. _____ view	9. _____ island
10. _____ book	11. _____ place	12. _____ ax
13. _____ cabin	14. _____ army	15. _____ berry
16. _____ puppy	17. _____ dream	18. _____ cousin
19. _____ museum	20. _____ show	21. _____ job
22. _____ train	23. _____ orange	24. _____ igloo
25. _____ exhibit	26. _____ box	27. _____ child
28. _____ hill	29. _____ fire	30. _____ mitten
31. _____ fork	32. _____ exit	33. _____ acorn
34. _____ crash	35. _____ kitchen	36. _____ shirt
37. _____ eye	38. _____ copy	39. _____ item
40. _____ sandwich	41. _____ month	42. _____ ostrich
43. _____ area	44. _____ fish	45. _____ airplane
46. _____ aquarium	47. _____ fly	48. _____ sled
49. _____ home	50. _____ walk	51. _____ game
52. _____ space	53. _____ olive	54. _____ mirror
55. _____ cup	56. _____ radio	57. _____ day
58. _____ umbrella	59. _____ ounce	60. _____ lion

Word Usage: lie and lay

Name _____

Date _____

Lesson 22

The word **lie** is a verb that means "to rest or recline." The forms of lie are **lie, lies, (is) lying, lay,** and **(have) lain.** Mark will **lie** on the sofa. Mark is **lying** on the sofa. He **lay** there for two hours. He has **lain** there for two hours.

The word **lay** is a verb that means "to put or place something." The forms of lay are **lay, lays, laying, laid,** and **(have, has, or had) laid.** Kathy, **lay** your coat on the bed. Kathy is **laying** her coat on the bed. She **laid** her coat on the bed. Kathy has **laid** the coat on the bed.

Write the correct form of the word **lie** or **lay** in each blank.

1. Peter and Zach _____ their towels on the sand.

2. "Zach, where have you _____ our picnic basket?" asked Peter.

3. "I _____ it under the umbrella," replied Zach.

4. Peter decided to _____ on his towel.

5. "How long has Peter been _____ on the sand?" asked Father.

6. "He has _____ there all afternoon," said Zach.

Write your own sentences using forms of **lie**.

7. lie(s): _____

8. lying: _____

9. lay: _____

10. lain: _____

Write your own sentences using forms of **lay**.

11. lay(s): _____

12. laying: _____

13. laid: _____

Word Usage: raise and rise

Lesson 23

The word **raise** is a verb that means to "grow something" or "move upward."

The forms of raise are **raise(s), (is) raising, raised,** and **have raised.** Ellen is **raising** the bottom shelf. We will **raise** tomatoes this year.

The word **rise** is a verb that means to "go up" or "get up." The forms of rise are **rise(s), (is) rising, rose,** and **(have) risen.** I **rise** at 6 each morning. The sun has **risen.**

Write the correct form of **raise** or **rise** in each blank.

1. The creek has _____ two inches.

2. Are you _____ watermelons this year?

3. Mother _____ the chair off the floor.

4. Tony _____ from his chair.

5. Nellie, will you _____ the shades?

6. We saw the smoke that _____ from the burning house.

7. Food prices are _____ rapidly.

8. Has David's temperature _____ since this morning?

That's using the old thinker!

Write your own sentences using forms of **raise**.

9. raise(s): _____

10. raising: _____

11. raised: _____

Write your own sentences using forms of **rise**.

12. rise(s): _____

13. rising: _____

14. rose: _____

15. risen: _____

Review Test 2

Lesson 24

You'll have a jump on it!

Name _____

Date _____

Tell whether each word is a **noun, pronoun,** or **verb.**

1. my _____
2. tree _____
3. run _____
4. ask _____
5. boy _____
6. their _____

Draw two lines under the **verb phrase** in each sentence.

7. The pitcher had thrown a curve ball.

8. Marty has read two chapters.

9. We could have done better.

10. Did you complete your assignment?

Draw one line under the **complete subject.**
Draw two lines under the **complete predicate.**

11. Natalie and I watched the parade.

12. Joey picked up the caterpillar.

13. Richard and Mom popped the popcorn.

Circle each **direct object.**
Draw one line under each **indirect object.**

14. Michael dropped the book.

15. I gave Melissa a birthday card.

16. Bill invited me to the movies.

Fill in the blanks with the correct words.

17. Mother squeezed _____lemon into the glass. (**a, an**)

18. Please _____the book on the counter. (**lay, lie**)

19. Rita is _____cucumbers this year. (**raising, rising**)

20. The sun has _____(**risen, raised**)

21. Jackie has been _____on the floor. (**laying, lying**)

Capitalization

Name _____

Date _____

Begin the names of places with a capital letter (**N**ew **J**ersey **T**urnpike, **U.S.** **H**ighway 101, **A**tlantic **O**cean, **R**ocky **M**ountains, **S**ilver **L**ake).

Begin the names of organizations, businesses, government bodies, and institutions with a capital letter (**L**eague of **W**omen **V**oters, **G**eneral **M**otors **C**orporation, **N**ogales **H**igh **S**chool, **H**illcrest **C**hurch, **H**ouse of **R**epresentatives).

Begin the names of sections of the country or the world with a capital letter (the **N**orth, the **F**ar **E**ast, the **M**idwest).

Do not capitalize these words when they refer to a direction (Turn **east** at the stoplight. He walked to the **north** side of the street.).

Circle the first letter of each word that should begin with a capital letter.

1. Where is the aegean sea located?

2. Alice traveled to riverside county on u.s. highway 10.

3. Mr. Jackson was elected to the senate for the second time.

4. Kim Lee is from the far east.

5. Roger belongs to the boy scouts of america.

6. Will your sister attend the university of michigan or stanford university?

7. Who is in charge of the department of agriculture?

8 Miss Ebbermyer has been working for american airlines.

9. Bobby crossed to the south side of fountain road.

10. Lupe and Freddy belong to our school's spanish club.

11. Is west virgina a separate state?

12. David and I walked to the whittwood theater last night.

You're doing a great job!

13. Tony attended a university in los angeles, california.

14. Those gentlemen are members of the veterans of foreign wars.

15. north america is very small compared to asia.

Capitalization and Punctuation

Name _____

Date _____

Lesson 26

Capitalize the first, last, and important words in the titles of books, stories, poems, songs, plays, and magazines.

Do not capitalize words like **a, an, and, at, by, for, in, of, the,** and **with,** unless they are the first word in the title.

Put quotation marks around the titles of songs, poems, stories, and plays when they are used in a sentence.

Underline the title of a book or magazine when it is used in a sentence.

Circle the first letter of each word that should begin with a capital letter. Use quotation marks and underlining in the right places.

1. Father purchased this month's copy of Reader's Digest.

2. Who has the book everybody's favorite ghost stories?

3. William Shakespeare wrote the play hamlet.

4. charlie and the chocolate factory is a book by Roald Dahl.

5. Aunt Vivian's favorite song is while strolling thru' the park one day.

6. Kathy read the book florence nightingale.

7. moon river is a romantic song.

8. Does Mr. Steiner still receive newsweek magazine?

9. No, he receives time magazine, Rodney.

10. when johnny comes marching home

Remember the rules!

11. Did Charles Dickens write the play a christmas carol?

12. national geographic magazine

13. Ali memorized the poem i walked through the forest.

14. ode to autumn is my favorite poem.

Pronouns: Subjects and Objects

Name _____

Date _____

Lesson 27

Use the pronouns **I, you, he, she, it, we,** and **they before a verb.** When used this way, they are called **subject pronouns.**

> **I** will come home.
> **You** and **he** tried to complete the project.
> **She** and **I** are good friends.
> **They** decided to stay home.
> **It** was fun!

Use the pronouns **me, you, him, her, it, us,** and **them after a verb.** When used this way, they are called **object pronouns.**

> Jackie told **me** about the trip.
> Henry will help **you** and **her.**
> Mother is going to talk to **her** and **me.**
> The Riners will go with **them.**
> Nancy held **it** all afternoon.

Notice that **you** and **it** can be used before or after the verb.

Tell whether the word in bold is an object pronoun or a subject pronoun. Write **object** or **subject** before each sentence.

1. _____ Sandy and **I** baked a cake.

2. _____ Will Roger and Elaine go with **them?**

3. _____ "I will be glad to help **you**," said Mother.

4. _____ **She** decided to work on the project tonight.

5. _____ Georgia will walk home with **her.**

6. _____ **They** are invited to my party.

7. _____ Teresa helped Joann and **me** pull weeds.

8. _____ "**You** are going to be late!" shouted Tony.

9. _____ **He** is the tallest boy in my class.

10. _____ Did you see **him** today?

11. _____ **It** was an exciting game!

12. _____ **We** have planned a surprise party for Paul.

13. _____ Will you help carry **it** home?

14. _____ Frankie thanked **us** for the ride.

It gets heavy but it's worth the effort!

Pronouns: Subjects and Objects

Lesson 28

Use the pronouns **I, you, he, she, it, we,** and **they before a verb.** When used this way, they are called **subject pronouns.**

Use the pronouns **me, you, him, her, it, us,** and **them after a verb.** When used this way, they are called **object pronouns.**

Circle the correct **pronoun(s)** in each sentence.

You're getting better and better!

1. Henry often plays basketball with Ricky and **I   me.**

2. **He   Him** watched the news three times yesterday.

3. Patsy and **we   us** took a ride.

4. **She   Her** is going to be a bridesmaid in **she   her** sister's wedding.

5. **They   Them** will come with **we   us.**

6. Will Father give **they   them** a ride home?

7. Roger and Carlos want **he   him** on their team.

8. **I   Me** will travel over the Rocky Mountains with **they   them.**

9. **She   Her** and **I   me** want to see that new movie.

10. Grandma gave Rachel and **I   me** a glass of lemonade.

11. Nancy will sit between you and **he   him.**

12. Mrs. Garcia told **she   her** that the cookies were delicious.

Write sentences using **you** and **it** as subject pronouns and object pronouns.

13. you (subject): _____

14. you (object): _____

15. it (subject): _____

16. it (object): _____

Pronouns and Contractions

Name _____

Date _____

Lesson 29

Some pronouns sound like contractions. (**Your** sounds like **you're**.)
To know which word to use, read the sentence using the contraction as two words.

Right: There's Bobby. (there is)
Wrong: Theirs Bobby.

Four pronouns and contractions that sound alike are

your and you're (you are)   its and it's (it is)
whose and who's (who is)   theirs and there's (there is)

Circle the right word in each sentence.

1. "**Who's Whose** car is parked in front of **you're your** house?" asked Jake.

2. **It's Its you're your** turn to wash the car.

3. **There's Theirs** a package waiting for **you're your** dad.

4. **Who's Whose** going to buy the popcorn?

5. **You're Your** a good friend.

6. The books are **there's theirs.**

7. Rita looked at the book and said, "Look at **it's its** cover."

8. **It's Its** going to be a hot day.

> It's as easy as falling off a log!

Use each word in a short sentence.

9. your: _____

10. you're: _____

11. theirs: _____

12. there's: _____

13. its: _____

14. it's: _____

15. whose: _____

16. who's: _____

Homonyms

Lesson 30

Name _____

Date _____

Homonyms are words that sound alike but have different meanings and spellings.

The wind **blew** my **blue** coat away.

You have learned about the homonyms **to, too, two, they're, their,** and **there.**

Write a sentence for each homonym below.

1. ate: past tense of eat	2. eight: the number 8
3. break: to destroy	4. brake: a device for stopping
5. cent: a penny or coin	6. sent: past tense of send
7. scent: a smell	8. dew: moisture on the ground
9. due: something owed	10. feat: an accomplishment
11. feet: plural of foot	12. feet: 12-inch measurements
13. flour: ground wheat	14. flower: a plant
15. heard: past tense of hear	16. herd: group of animals

1. _____

2. _____

3. _____

4. _____

5. _____

6. _____

7. _____

8. _____

9. _____

10. _____

11. _____

12. _____

13. _____

14. _____

15. _____

16. _____

Homonyms
Lesson 31

Name _____

Date _____

Homonyms are words that sound alike but have different meanings and spellings. **(ate - eight, heard - herd, scent - sent - cent)**

Circle the correct word(s) in each sentence.

1. Marcia put her **feat feet** into the icy water.

2. My library book was **dew due** last **week weak.**

3. Did those **ate eight flowers flours** come from your yard?

4. Frances **scent sent scent** her **aunt ant** a birthday card.

5. **Too To Two** dollars is a **fare fair** price.

6. Thomas walked down the long **hall haul** and turned **write right rite.**

7. Mother loves the **sent cent scent** of a freshly picked **rows rose.**

8. Jess hurt his large **toe tow** when he **rowed road rode** his skateboard.

9. When did Lena **sow so sew** that **knew new** dress?

10. Karen went to **see sea** the **principal principle.**

11. Use good **stationary stationery** to **right write rite** your letter.

12. Juan's father was a **kernel colonel** in the army.

13. Orson drew a **strait straight** line across that **piece peace** of **would wood.**

14. Yolanda **through threw** the **pair pare pear** of skates over the fence.

15. Who made the **whole hole** in this **pail pale**?

16. What kind of **serial cereal** did you have this morning?

17. The bank **maid made** three hundred dollars on this **lone loan.**

18. **They're There Their** answer is **know no.**

Adjectives

Don't give up! You're doing great!

Lesson 32

Name _____

Date _____

An **adjective** is a word that describes a noun or pronoun. It describes **"what kind," "which one,"** or **"how many."**

Frederick wore **leather** gloves.

In this sentence, leather is an adjective describing gloves. Leather tells what kind of gloves Frederick wore.

Write a short sentence using each adjective with the word it describes.

1. slippery floor: _____

2. two giraffes: _____

3. frightened child:_____

4. blue sky: _____

5. kind man: _____

6. all of them: _____

7. sweet ice cream: _____

8. fluffy frosting: _____

9. almost everyone: _____

10. gentle kitten: _____

11. black smoke: _____

12. that barn: _____

13. several lemons: _____

14. tiny ant: _____

15. windy day: _____

16. only him: _____

17. happy baby: _____

18. wet newspaper: _____

19. sparkling jewels: _____

20. this house: _____

Adjectives

Lesson 33

Name _____

Date _____

An **adjective** is a word that describes a noun or pronoun.
It describes "**what kind**," "**which one**," or "**how many**."

This man walks to work each day.
The **black** cat hid in the corner.
Most children in this room are ten.
Two ducks jumped in the water.

Circle each adjective. Underline the word being described.

1. Every child rides a bus.

2. The tired hikers rested by the stream.

3. The talkative group enjoyed the party.

4. The old barn fell apart during the storm.

5. We watched the frail bird hop into the bushes.

6. Almost everyone came to school.

7. Several oranges fell off the fruit stand.

8. Marta ate the crisp and crunchy cereal.

9. Did you see the rough and rugged cowboy?

10. Mother gave us buttered toast.

11. The bright sunshine warmed the room.

12. We watched the tall, dark, and handsome man enter that bank.

13. The silly joke made the children laugh.

14. Danny's terrified puppy hid under the couch.

15. Elsa shouted, "Watch the dangerous curve ahead!"

16. This movie costs seven dollars.

17. Vera used the difficult spelling words in sentences.

18. Regina pulled the tattered and torn curtains off the rods.

Hurray! You're going to come out on top!

Adverbs

Lesson 34

Name _____

Date _____

An **adverb** is a word that describes a verb, adjective, or other adverb. It usually tells **when, how, where,** or **how often** something is done.

The kitten jumped **quickly** off the bed.

Write a short sentence using each adverb with the word it describes.

1. drive carefully: _____

2. waited patiently: _____

3. jogged slowly: _____

4. finished easily: _____

5. ate quickly: _____

6. spoke softly: _____

7. opened suddenly: _____

8. displayed proudly: _____

9. ran fastest: _____

10. walked quicker: _____

11. written badly: _____

12. came here: _____

13. was nearby: _____

14. merrily sang: _____

15. often read: _____

16. traveled farther: _____

17. left yesterday: _____

18. jumped high: _____

19. slept peacefully: _____

20. worked quietly: _____

Adverbs

Lesson 35

Name _____

Date _____

An **adverb** is a word that describes a verb, adjective, or other adverb. It usually tells **how, when, where,** or **how often** something is done.

Nancy ran **quickly**.
Rusty will come **tomorrow**.
Henry threw the ball **there**.
Mother cooks **creatively**.

Circle each adverb. Underline the word(s) being described.

1. My friends slept here.

2. Team A ran fastest.

3. Did Pete leave at seven?

4. Billy shouted the instructions loudly.

5. Lupe and I proudly showed our awards.

6. The baby played quietly.

7. The door flew open suddenly.

8. Allison swims easily.

9. Jesse is an unusually good student.

10. Greg takes boxing lessons every Tuesday and Thursday.

11. Our plane landed safely.

12. Kathy and Mindy are working hard.

13. Mike can almost ride a unicycle.

14. He talked nonstop.

15. Mrs. Pauley predicted the outcome accurately.

16. Mr. and Mrs. Wentz made the announcement recently.

17. Father seldom has a meeting on Tuesday.

18. Charlie boldly raised his hand.

You're getting the "drift" of it!

Circle the first letter of each word that should begin with a capital letter.

1. my family and I traveled through the south last may.

2. we flew to texas on continental airlines.

3. gilbert and I had a picnic east of willow creek.

4. joseph attended rutgers university.

Circle the first letter of each word that should begin with a capital letter.
Use underlining and quotation marks in the right places.

5. I read the book little women in the fifth grade.

6. Maria wrote a poem called my favorite friend and i.

7. sports illustrated

8. Mother receives family circle every month.

Tell whether the word in bold type is an object pronoun or a subject pronoun.
Write **object** or **subject** on each line.

9. _____ Mary and **I** delivered the newspapers.

10. _____ Frankie gave Cindy and **me** a bag of peppermint.

11. _____ **It** is a wonderful day!

12. _____ She sent **him** a present.

Circle the correct word(s) in each sentence.

13. The **scent cent** of the freshly picked **flowers flours** filled the air.

14. Terry bought a **pair pare pear** and **too two to** oranges.

Tell whether the word in bold is an adjective or an adverb.
Write **Adjective** or **Adverb** on each line.

15. _____ **Seven** children played tag.

16. _____ Tommy sat **patiently** in the doctor's office.

17. _____ Randy slipped on the **wet** floor.

18. _____ What a **beautiful** jacket!

19. _____ We ran **quickly** across the street.

That's using the old thinker!

Complete Subjects and Simple Subjects

Name _____

Date _____

Lesson 37

Every sentence has two parts: the **subject** and the **predicate.** The **complete subject** consists of all the words in the sentence that describe what or who is being talked about.

> **The little girl with long brown hair** is my niece.

The **simple subject** is the main word in the complete subject. The simple subject is usually a noun or pronoun.

> The little **girl** with long brown hair is my niece.

Draw one line under the complete subject. Circle the simple subject. The first one is an example.

1. The fortieth (president) of the United States of America was Ronald Wilson Reagan.

2. The tired kitten curled up in front of the warm fireplace.

3. Nancy washed the dishes after lunch.

4. That tall boy might become a good basketball player.

5. The billowing black smoke could be seen for miles.

6. Pretty pink streamers hung from the ceiling.

7. The cool night air felt good after a long hot day.

8. The large spider plant hung over the patio entrance.

That's it! You're going to get it!

9. Jackie will run in her first race on Monday, June 10.

10. Rusty stayed after school for baseball practice.

11. A guided tour of the Los Angeles County Museum was about to begin.

12. Lori practiced playing the piano all morning.

13. Our school band is marching in the parade tomorrow.

14. Two brown buttons were missing from the jacket sleeves.

15. Our public library is not open on Sunday.

16. Many people will visit the new city park.

Complete Predicates and Predicate Verbs

Name _____

Date _____

Lesson 38

Every sentence has two parts: the **subject** and the **predicate.**
The **complete predicate** consists of all the words in the sentence that describe what the subject is doing, did, or will do.

My brother **ran home from school today.**

The **predicate verb** is the main verb or verb phrase in the complete predicate.

My brother **ran** home from school today.

Draw two lines under the complete predicate. Circle the predicate verb. The first one is an example.

1. Larry (jumped) onto the rock near the water's edge.

2. Joan and I cheered for our favorite team.

3. Chris dropped one more quarter into the machine.

4. The clerk examined the jacket carefully.

5. Margie's dog, Bandit, is a frisky animal.

6. My teacher asked for volunteers.

7. The birds ate all the seeds.

8. Rex and I are in the same race.

9. Some plants, like the fern, cannot make their own seeds.

10. Father purchased a new saw and hammer.

11. Francine threw the newspaper in the trash can.

12. Jody has moved to Lincoln, Kentucky.

13. Father will help cook dinner tonight.

14. My family and I flew to Arizona on Wednesday.

15. Gina carried her blue umbrella to school.

16. The boys are learning a new magic trick.

That's the trick!

Conjunctions

Name _____

Date _____

A **conjunction** is a word that joins two or more words or groups of words. The words **and, or, but,** and **for** are common conjunctions.

Wendy **and** I stayed home.
Ricky can play tennis **or** soccer.
I baked cookies, **but** no one ate any.
I gave Paul a birthday card, **for** he is my friend.

Circle the conjunction in each sentence.

1. Mother took both Sally and me to the movies.

2. Bring your hat and coat.

3. Elsa must clear the table and wash the dishes.

4. Are you and he best friends?

5. I ran quickly, but didn't make it to the store in time.

6. You may have pie or ice cream for dessert.

7. Robert made the basketball and baseball teams.

8. Miriam won first prize, for she is a good cook.

9. I rang the doorbell, but no one answered.

10. We had pork chops and mashed potatoes for dinner.

11. Did you lose it at the park or at school?

12. Mary finished last, but was a good sport.

13. Cliff does yardwork for Mr. Wagner and Mr. Hayes.

14. Will you help me with the math and spelling homework?

Hurray for you!

Write a sentence using each conjunction.

15. and: _____

16. for: _____

17. but: _____

18. or: _____

         FS123255 Skill Drill Grammar Grades 4–5

Compound Subjects and Conjunctions

Name _____

Date _____

Lesson 40

The **subject** tells what or who is being talked about.

Sally went shopping.

A **compound subject** consists of two or more subject words.
Conjunctions like **and** or **or** usually connect compound subjects.

Sally and **I** went shopping.

Sally, Jean, and **I** went shopping.

You're catching on now!

Draw a line under the **compound subject.**
Circle the **conjunction** in each sentence.

1. Two blouses and a skirt were purchased by the girls.

2. Peanuts and raisins are my favorite snack.

3. Mother and Aunt Rita will arrive shortly.

4. Either Terry or Patty will plant the corn.

5. The books and magazines are neatly stacked in the corner.

6. Clifton and I watched the game on television.

7. Coffee, tea, and milk were served on the airplane.

8. A dog, cat, and boy were seen chasing the car.

9. Bobby and his family moved to Wisconsin.

10. Swimming and jogging are my favorite activities.

11. Milk, butter, and eggs are needed in this recipe.

12. A doctor or a nurse will give the shot.

13. My friend and I built a model airplane.

14. Tomatoes, carrots, and cucumbers were planted this year.

Write your own sentences with compound subjects using **and** and **or.**

15. and: _____

16. or: _____

Compound Predicates and Conjunctions

Name _____

Date _____

Lesson 41

The **predicate verb** is the word(s) that tells what the subject is doing, did, or will do.

John **swam** three laps across the pool.

A **compound predicate** consists of two or more predicate verbs.
Conjunctions like **and** or **or** usually connect compound predicates.

John **swam** and **jogged** this afternoon.
Amy **scrubbed, mopped,** and **waxed** the kitchen floor.

Draw two lines under the **compound predicate.**
Circle the **conjunction** in each sentence.

1. Ricky went in the house and opened the package.

2. Father cut and watered the lawn.

3. Ida tripped over the rock and hurt her ankle.

4. Heather typed and studied the spelling list.

5. Mother will bake or buy the cookies.

6. We stopped at the pizzeria and ordered a pizza.

7. Nancy may trim the roses or plant new flowers.

8. Cindy purchased balloons and filled them with water.

9. Barry dove into the water and swam across the pool.

10. I baked, cut, and served the birthday cake.

11. The teacher erased the board and wrote a new problem.

12. Karen washed and waxed Father's car.

13. Tommy sliced, toasted, and buttered the bread.

14. Maria will sing and dance tonight.

Don't let it bog you down!

Write your own sentences with compound predicates using **and** and **or.**

15. and: _____

16. or: _____

Compound Sentences and Conjunctions

Name _____

Date _____

Lesson 42

A **compound sentence** is made up of two complete thoughts (simple sentences) joined by a conjunction.

Two simple sentences:
   Mrs. Steiner is known as a poet. She sings and dances.

Compound sentence:
   Mrs. Steiner is known as a poet, **but** she can also sing and dance.

Complete each sentence. Use the conjunctions **and, or, for,** or **but** after the comma. Remember, the second part must contain a subject and a predicate.

1. The sky is blue, _____

2. My father went shopping, _____

3. The doorbell rang, _____

4. Kim Lee returned home, _____

5. Complete your homework, _____

6. He walked into the office, _____

7. You may buy the shirt, _____

8. We went swimming, _____

9. Mr. Garza asked a question, _____

10. I can go to the game, _____

11. Why not ask your parents, _____

12. Some athletes are paid well, _____

13. Mrs. Charleton told us, _____

14. Sandra boarded the airplane, _____

15. We walked home, _____

16. He can read and write French, _____

17. Lisa made the team, _____

18. Thomas bought the milk, _____

Prepositions

Lesson 43

A **preposition** is a connecting word. It connects ideas.
A preposition also shows the relationship between a noun or a pronoun to some other word or idea in the sentence.

He left the book **on** the desk.
Wilma stayed **after** school.
Tina walked **behind** the car.
We were late **on** account **of** his tardiness.

A preposition can be a single word or two or more words. There are many prepositions. Some prepositions are **to, in, at, by, on, for, from, with, under, over, above, among, between, behind, after, toward, due to, on account of,** and **because of.**

Each sentence below contains a preposition. Circle it.

1. I left my books at school.

2. Alex came by my house.

3. Did you see the man on the corner?

4. Adrian peeked in the window.

5. Fred, Larry, and Tim jogged toward the lake.

6. I studied with Marty today.

7. On account of the show, school was canceled.

8. Father's slippers were under the sofa.

9. You may have ice cream after dinner.

10. Cindy put cheese between the slices of meat.

11. The boys divided the pencils among themselves.

12. The kite flew above the tree tops.

13. Wendy and Steve walked to the store.

14. Leslie picked roses from her garden.

15. What is in that large package?

16. Jeff kicked the ball over the fence.

17. It was due to her good grades.

18. John's puppy ran behind the house.

Hang in there!

Prepositions
Lesson 44

A **preposition** is a connecting word. It connects ideas.
A preposition also shows the relationship between a noun or pronoun to some other word or idea in the sentence.

A preposition may show **time, cause, direction,** or **position.**

Time: before, after, during, until, while, since
Cause: on account of, in spite of, due to, because of, since
Direction: across, toward, from, around, behind
Position: above, against, beneath, on, over, under, inside

Tell whether the preposition in bold shows time, cause, direction, or position.
Write **time, cause, direction,** or **position** on each line.

1. _____ Randy hid the package **under** his pillow.

2. _____ Teresa rode her bicycle **toward** us.

3. _____ **In spite of** the rain, we walked to school

4. _____ Marilyn stayed **in** her room all afternoon.

5. _____ The students did not talk **during** the test.

6. _____ Write your name **on** this paper.

7. _____ We finished our work **before** going swimming.

8. _____ **Because of** her behavior, she stayed home.

9. _____ Mr. Elsberg lives **around** the corner.

10. _____ We took a nap **under** the tree.

11. _____ Did you see the helicopter fly **over** us?

12. _____ Liz set the table, **while** I prepared dinner.

13. _____ I can't go, **since** I didn't finish my chores.

14. _____ Darrell walked **into** the principal's office.

15. _____ We studied **during** the lunch hour.

16. _____ I haven't practiced **since** yesterday.

17. _____ Linda took a can of peas **from** the shelf.

18. _____ Does Jill take tap lessons **after** school?

Prepositional Phrases

Lesson 45

Name _____

Date _____

A **prepositional phrase** is a group of words starting with a preposition. The phrase usually ends with a noun or pronoun.

> I heard the news **on the radio.**
> Rita reached **into the bag.**

A sentence may have more than one prepositional phrase.

> I listened **to the news   on the radio.**
> Rita reached **into the bag   for an apple.**

Draw a line under each prepositional phrase.
Circle the preposition beginning each phrase.

1. Did Mark move to Salt Lake City?

2. While we watched the movie, Nora left to buy popcorn.

3. Roy and Otis are in my science class.

4. Uncle Max will arrive within the hour.

5. Did you see the accident at Hollywood and Vine?

6. The cute little girl in the pink dress sings in the choir.

7. We walked among the trees.

8. Greg took the glass of milk from Lucy.

9. Anita and Claudia were kept after school.

10. The parade began behind the department store.

11. The plate of spaghetti slipped from my hands.

12. We danced to the music of the new band.

13. Sonny is at Grandma's house.

14. Due to Washington's birthday, we will stay home.

15. The children rode their bicycles up the street.

16. We built sand castles near the seashore.

You're on your way!

FS123255 Skill Drill Grammar Grades 4–5

Pronouns:
Subject and Object

Name _____

Date _____

Lesson 46

Use the pronouns **I, you, he, she, it, we,** and **they** before a verb. When used this way, they are called **subject pronouns.**

Use the pronouns **me, you, him, her, it, us,** and **them** after a verb. When used this way, they are called **object pronouns.**

Write your own sentences using each pronoun.

Subject Pronouns

1. I: _____

2. you: _____

3. he: _____

4. she: _____

5. it: _____

6. we: _____

7. they: _____

Object Pronouns

8. me: _____

9. you: _____

10. him: _____

11. her: _____

12. it: _____

13. us: _____

14. them: _____

Tell whether the pronoun in bold is a subject pronoun or an object pronoun. Write **subject** or **object** on the lines.

15. _____ You and **I** will be on the same team.

16. _____ Ralph took **it** away from Dorothy.

Pronouns:
Singular and Relative

Lesson 47

When a singular pronoun is followed by another pronoun, the second pronoun must also be singular. The following words are troublesome singular pronouns:

someone	anyone	everyone	none	each
somebody	anybody	everybody	nobody	everything

Everybody has finished **his** assignment.
Has **anyone** completed **his** dinner?

The pronouns **that, which,** and **who** are called **relative pronouns.**

Use **who** when speaking of **people.**
   The girl who arrived is my sister.

Use **which** when including extra information about **animals** or **things** that is not needed to understand the sentence. Set off these **which** phrases with commas.
   His dog, which is a Dalmatian, has won many awards.

Use **that** when speaking of **people, things,** or **animals.**
   The house that we live in has been painted blue.

Circle the correct pronoun in each sentence.

1. Did someone lose **their his** skates?

2. The man **who which** walked by is our principal.

3. Is he the boy **who which** won the race?

4. Can anyone swim on **their his** back?

5. Somebody left **their his** books on the counter.

6. Fluffy is a cat **who that** loves to scratch.

7. At the Women's Club meeting everyone received **their her** membership card.

8. Our teacher asked the students **which that** disturbed the class to stay after school.

9. The horse **who that** won received the trophy.

10. Fred is a boy **who which** studies hard every night.

11. One of the children **who which** came to the party forgot his jacket.

12. None of the swimmers completed **their his** required laps.

13. This puppy **who which** belongs to my uncle, needs a bath.

14. Mrs. Simon, the lady **who which** spoke to our class, is my aunt.

48   FS123255 Skill Drill Grammar Grades 4–5

Interjections

Lesson 48

An **interjection** is a word that shows strong feeling:
Ouch! Oh! Well! Great! Aha! Alas! Hurrah! Please!
Sometimes an interjection is a short phrase: **Watch out! Of course! Not on your life!**

An interjection begins with a capital letter, ends in an exclamation point, and is separate from a sentence.

Some words that are used as interjections are also used in sentences to show mild feeling: Oh, **shucks**, I dropped my books. When used this way, they are **not** interjections.

Circle each interjection. Put an exclamation point after each interjection.

1. Look out The wagon is tipping!

2. Alas

3. I have completed the assignment at last.

4. Slow down We don't have to be there for another hour.

5. For goodness sake

6. Hurrah Our team scored another point!

7. Aha I saw you eat the last cookie.

8. Look Here comes Linda.

9. But, gosh, we won't be able to watch the show.

10. No way

11. Please Sit in your chairs.

12. Bah I won't touch it!

13. Cheers We have a great Mom!

14. All right I'll let you have the basketball.

15. I'm, oh, so glad you found the little girl.

16. Watch out The train is coming.

17. Stop it Danny and I won't help you!

18. Oh my gosh

You're doing a great job!

Sentences

Name _____

Date _____

There are **four kinds of sentences.**

1. A **declarative** sentence makes a statement. It should end in a period.
   (Karen plays basketball.)

2. An **imperative** sentence gives a command. It should end in a period.
   (Karen, come here.)

3. An **interrogative** sentence asks a question. It should end in a question mark.
   (Where is Karen?)

4. An **exclamatory** sentence shows surprise or strong emotion. It should end in an exclamation point.
   (Karen's team won!)

Write **declarative, imperative, interrogative**, or **exclamatory** on each line. Put the right punctuation mark at the end of each sentence.

1. _____ What a great game

2. _____ Who answered the door

3. _____ David's birthday is next Saturday

4. _____ Sammy, bring me the basket

5. _____ Look at that strange animal

6. _____ What a wonderful party

7. _____ Why did Mrs. Lim call

8. _____ Tell me about the race, Father

9. _____ My little brother takes a nap every day

10. _____ Rachel studied until nine last night

Write your own sentences.

11. declarative: _____

12. imperative: _____

13. interrogative: _____

14. exclamatory: _____

Don't give up! You're doing great!

Name _____

Date _____

Draw a line under the **simple subject** and two lines under the **predicate verb.**

1. The boy in the brown jacket ran home from school.

2. Peter will help Father trim the roses.

Draw a line under each subject and two lines under each **predicate.**
Circle each **conjunction.**

3. Jackie and I enrolled in the gymnastics class.

4. Roberta sang and played the piano.

5. Roses, carnations, and daisies are my favorite flowers.

6. Kathy may buy or make a skirt.

7. Allen jogged, swam, and played tennis last week.

Draw a line under each **prepositional phrase.**
Circle the **preposition** beginning each phrase.

8. Due to bad weather, the game has been cancelled.

9. Ben placed his books on the counter.

10. Larry studied at the library.

Circle the correct **pronoun.**

11. **Her She** gave Kathy and **I me** a ride to school.

12. The horse **who that** won the race belongs to Mr. Keats.

13. Nobody studied for **their his** test.

14. Professor Daniels, the man **who which** just arrived, is an excellent speaker.

Write **declarative, imperative, interrogative,** or **exclamatory** on each blank line. Use periods, question marks, and exclamation points.

15. _____ Did you see my new surfboard

16. _____ Jackie, please help me carry the plates

17. _____ My father is being transferred to Ohio

18. _____ What a great game

Capitalization Review

Lesson 51

Name _____

Date _____

Circle the first letter of each word that should begin with a capital letter.

1. one week before the winter break, mrs. j. adams asked her class to decorate the room for christmas.

2. "someday i will become a famous artist," said steven.

3. this reminded mrs. adams of a story in <u>highlights</u> magazine.

Use capital letters.

4. she decided to read the story "norman rockwell: the illustrator everyone knows" to her class.

5. when mrs. adams finished reading the story, they reviewed what they had learned.

6. norman rockwell was a world-famous illustrator.

7. his eighth-grade teacher, miss smith, encouraged norman in his drawing.

8. during his first year in high school, norman took art lessons every wednesday and friday.

9. norman took art lessons at the chase school of art in new york.

10. when he turned sixteen, norman studied at the national academy school.

11. edward cave, the editor of <u>boys' life</u> magazine, gave norman a job as an illustrator.

12. mr. rockwell sold his first magazine cover to the <u>saturday evening post.</u>

13. he also illustrated the books <u>tom sawyer</u>, <u>huckleberry finn</u>, and <u>louisa may alcott: america's best loved writer.</u>

14. every year norman rockwell painted a picture for the boy scout calendar.

15. mr. rockwell's art studio in arlington, vermont, burned down in 1943.

16. "i really enjoyed the story, mrs. adams," said steven.

17. "my favorite illustration is the one of the thanksgiving day meal," said loretta.

18. the children then talked about special holidays celebrated by the irish, french, and chinese.

Punctuation Review

Lesson 52

Name _____

Date _____

Use periods, question marks, exclamation points, commas, quotation marks, apostrophes, and underlining in the right places.

1. Mrs L Jacobson moved to 332 Pine Street on April 13 1981

2. Denise what is your new address

3. My new address is 505 Rose Avenue Culver City California

4. Look out

5. Paul Michael and Dean formed a singing group

6. Yes we will attend the meeting

7. Hasnt he been there before

8. Ians sister is Yolandas best friend

9. The title of my poem is By the Seaside

Hurray! You're going to come out on top!

10. Does your brother still receive Sesame Street Magazine

11. Becky please come here said Mother

12. Roger said Dr Franco is our new principal

13. On June 18 1995 my grandparents traveled to Melbourne Australia to visit my Uncle Jacob

14. Your dogs collar needs to be replaced

15. That girls dress is beautiful

16. Will you asked Mother be home before nine

17. Were going to Pats house Dad

18. Irenes friend lives on Lemon Avenue said Michelle

19. Our team won

20. Judge Samuel T Swenson wont be in court today

21. Aha

22. No Randy Ill be away on September 19 said Corrine

Word Usage Review

Lesson 53

Name _____

Date _____

Circle the correct word(s) in each sentence.

1. My **father's   fathers'** car is newly painted.

2. We plan to visit Uncle Harry in **won   one   week   weak.**

3. Does **a   an** apple   **a   an** day really keep the doctor away?

4. Olivia is **laying   lying** on the sofa.

5. Ben is **raising   rising** sunflowers in the backyard.

6. **Men's   Mens'** jackets are on **sail   sale** today.

7. **A   An** accident occurred at the track **meet   meat.**

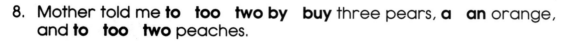

That's using the old thinker!

8. Mother told me **to   too   two by   buy** three pears, **a   an** orange, and **to   too   two** peaches.

9. **Lay   Lie** your books on the table.

10. Her **child's   childs'** sister has been ill.

11. **Cindy's   Cindys'** papers **blew   blue** away in the wind.

12. Paul **lay   laid** on the grass and watching the smoke from the chimney **raise   rise** into the air.

Write the contraction for each pair of words.

13. who is _____ 14. you are _____ 15. there is _____

16. could not _____ 17. I am _____ 18. we will _____

Write a synonym and an antonym for each word. Use each word from the list only once.

| energetic | light | large | dark |
| small | tired | simple | difficult |

	Synonym	**Antonym**
19. gigantic	_____	_____
20. pale	_____	_____
21. lively	_____	_____
22. easy	_____	_____

Sentence Review
Lesson 54

Name _____

Date _____

Write **declarative, imperative, exclamatory,** or **interrogative** on the line before each sentence. Use periods, question marks, and exclamation points.

1. _____ Did you watch the parade

2. _____ Ouch! That hurt

3. _____ You are wonderful

4. _____ Mrs. Fisher will be our new teacher

5. _____ Start walking, Mike

6. _____ How did you do on the math test

7. _____ The girls won the game

8. _____ Summer vacation begins tomorrow

9. _____ May I borrow this dictionary

10. _____ Aha! I caught you

Change each sentence fragment into a good sentence. Change each run-on into a good sentence. Use capital letters and end punctuation in the right places.

11. Ginger and I. _____

12. All the girls in the audience. _____

13. Cora went swimming, I wanted to go too. _____

_____

14. While I washed my hair. _____

15. Pepper jumped on the sofa, Mother took her down. _____

_____

16. Jean washed the car, Allison dried it. _____

_____

17. In order to have plenty of food to eat at the picnic. _____

_____

Name _____

Date _____

Circle each **common noun**. Underline each **proper noun**.

1. Sylvia met me at Hubbard's Department Store.

2. We took a spelling test and math test last Thursday.

3. Grant Avenue crosses Lincoln Boulevard near my house.

Draw two lines under each **verb** or **verb phrase**.

4. Charlene will speak to our club members this evening.

5. Are the children coming to the picnic?

6. Bobby slept for twelve hours!

Underline each **direct object**. Circle each **indirect object**.

7. Mike gave Kathy a red rose.

8. I told Susan about our vacation.

9. Grandma baked banana bread.

10. Carol and I used the new computer.

11. Pearl handed Christine the bread basket.

Keep moving! You're doing GREAT!

Underline each **prepositional phrase**. Circle the **preposition**.

12. Henry met me at the creek.

13. William put the socks in his shoes.

14. Due to the strike Mr. James did not work today.

15. The children marched under the bridge.

16. Frisky ran around the house and over the fence.

Circle each **interjection**.

17. Alas! There's no hope left for me.

18. Hold it! I'll take over for you.

Subject, Predicate, and Conjunction Review

Name _____

Date _____

Lesson 56

Draw one line under the **simple subject**. Draw two lines under the **predicate verb**.

1. Norman Rockwell painted a self-portrait.

2. My friend Melissa lives on Hyatt Avenue.

3. Leslie is preparing the hamburgers.

4. The man in the yellow jacket is directing traffic.

Draw one line under each **subject**. Draw two lines under each **predicate verb**. Circle each **conjunction**.

5. John, Sam, and I wrote the school play.

6. Either Mary or Nanette will play the lead part.

7. I read my book and wrote the report last night.

8. California and Texas are large states.

It's as easy as falling off a log!

Circle the **conjunctions**.

9. Jennifer returned home, for it was late.

10. The teacher asked a question, but no one answered.

11. You may buy the skirt or the shoes.

12. Blythe invited Ellen and Ken to her party.

13. Tina and I ate pizza and jogged around the block.

14. Sara tried calling Hank on the telephone, but the line was busy.

Write your own sentences.

15. compound subject: _____

16. compound predicate: _____

17. compound sentence: _____

18. compound subject and predicate: _____

_____

Pronoun Review

Lesson 57

Name _____

Date _____

Circle the **pronouns.**

1. My friend and I visited our teacher at her home.

2. We will walk to the creek and meet them at their campsite.

3. They will take it to your house before bringing it to mine.

Tell whether the word in bold is a subject or object pronoun. Write **subject** or **object** before each sentence.

4. _____ He and **I** won first prize in the art contest.

5. _____ Vincent promised to walk home with **her.**

6. _____ **It** was a great party!

7. _____ Mom put **it** on the top shelf.

You're getting the "drift" of it!

Circle the correct **pronoun.**

8. Lorraine and **she   her** entered the speech contest.

9. Please sit next to **he   him.**

10. **We   Us** girls are on the track team.

11. **Who's   Whose** going to try out for the school play?

12. Somebody forgot **their   his** jacket at school.

13. The animal **who   that** made these tracks has a broken leg.

14. Mother told **she   her** to pack the suitcase.

15. The Elliott family thanked **we   us** for inviting them.

16. The package **who   that** arrived yesterday is for **he   him.**

17. Tracy gave Julie and **I   me** guitar lessons.

18. **They   Them** invited **we   us** to come with **they   them.**

19. Andy and **I   me** are learning to play chess.

20. The blue car is **there's   theirs.**

21. Lloyd, the boy **which   that** was on television, moved last week.

© Frank Schaffer Publications, Inc.   58   FS123255 Skill Drill Grammar Grades 4–5

Adjective and Adverb Review

Lesson 58

Don't let it bog you down!

Circle each **adjective**. Underline each **adverb**.

1. Father removed the splinter carefully.

2. Bright and early one morning, I went for a hike.

3. The soft and luxurious sofa was on display.

4. Thomas lightly buttered the crispy toast.

5. The moody students were behaving selfishly.

6. Martina's white lace blouse was made by her aunt.

7. The ball rolled slowly down the hill.

8. Larry walked into the dark and mysterious cave.

9. Jill and her tired family left Yosemite National Park **yesterday**.

10. Father worked quietly in the cozy office.

Write the **noun** or **verb** that the word in bold is describing.

11. _____ The **tiny** ant crawled up her sleeve.

12. _____ I found a **bright,** new penny.

13. _____ I **often** read before going to bed.

14. _____ **This** house was built by his father.

15. _____ **Gentle** rain fell against my face.

16. _____ **Lovely** flowers seemed to be everywhere.

17. _____ Anna used her mother's **silk** handkerchief.

18. _____ The window shattered **suddenly.**

19. _____ The Hartley family moved **here** in May.

20. _____ Our **kind** neighbor gave Betsy a ride.

Capitalization, Punctuation, and Sentences Test

Name _____

Date _____

Lesson 59

Circle the first letter of each word that should begin with a capital letter. Use punctuation marks in the correct places.

1. rj smith moved to the north end of meadowlark avenue

2. my friends dog, annabell, had puppies on march 3 1998

3. nonsense im not going to do it exclaimed george

4. when my uncle, dr kenneth johnson, came to visit on thanksgiving day, we sang america the beautiful

5. larry jimmy and brad deliver newspapers in manchester new hampshire on monday wednesday and friday

6. elizabeths grandmother, who lives in the east, collects santa clara native american pottery

7. did nora and irene join the girl scouts of america last january

8. while in france, aunt rachel learned to make fine french pastry

9. gil would you run a few errands for me asked mrs lee

10. teddys favorite book is i love you, dear dragon

11. andy said jerry and i will camp at yellowstone national park during the memorial day weekend

12. oh dont you also receive inside sports magazine

You're getting better and better!

Identify each type of sentence. Write **declarative, imperative, interrogative, exclamatory, fragment,** or **run-on** on each line.

13. _____ Over the hill and beyond the valley.

14. _____ Father will be home soon.

15. _____ Bill, come here at once.

16. _____ Mother and I prepared dinner, I didn't want to eat.

17. _____ What a wonderful idea!

18. _____ May I borrow two eggs and a cup of milk?

Word Usage Test

Lesson 60

Name _____

Date _____

Circle the correct word(s) in each sentence.

1. **A   An** airplane flew **threw   through** the cloudy sky.

2. Is **he   him** the same man **who   which** wrote this article?

3. **She   Her** is **raising   rising** the books to the top shelf.

4. The sun will **raise   rise** by five tomorrow morning.

5. Mother purchased **too   to   two   pairs   pares   pears** of shoes.

6. Frisky is the same cat **who   that** was caught in the tree.

7. **He   Him   raised   rose** from the bed on which **he   him** was **laying   lying.**

8. Helen thanked **we   us** for giving **her   she** a nice party.

9. Jan and **I   me** will meet **they   them** at the station.

10. **We   Us** parents plan to **see   sea   hour   our** children in **there   their** play.

11. **Who's   Whose** books are **laying   lying** on the table?

12. **They   Them** helped **I   me** wash Father's car.

Write your own sentences using each word.

13. a: _____

14. an: _____

15. any form of lay: _____

16. any form of lie: _____

17. any form of raise: _____

18. any form of rise: _____

Write a **synonym** for each word.

19. picture _____   20. enemy _____   21. tiny_____

Write an **antonym** for each word.

22. wild_____   23. win_____   24. slowly _____

Parts of Speech Test

Name _____

Date _____

What part of speech is the word in bold type in each sentence?
Write **noun, verb, pronoun, adjective, adverb, preposition, conjunction,** or **interjection** on each line.

1. _____ A fire began **behind** the cafeteria.

2. _____ **Frances** delivered the homemade bread.

3. _____ A gust of wind blew the **dry** leaves into the street.

4. _____ The recipe called for two cups of **flour.**

5. _____ **We** took them to the airport.

6. _____ Ellen **will be running** in today's race.

7. _____ Vera worked **slowly** and carefully.

8. _____ **Ouch**! I burned my finger.

9. _____ **Due to** your poor grades, you'll have to study harder.

10. _____ We wanted apple pie, **but** Mother baked cookies.

11. _____ Stop! That blue car almost hit **us**!

12. _____ **Twenty-five** students passed the test.

Underline each **direct object**. Circle each **indirect object.**

13. Alice told Janet a secret.

14. Billy mailed the package.

Underline each **subject pronoun**. Circle each **object pronoun.**

15. Jimmy and I went to the movies with her.

16. We thanked Mr. Fredrick.

Underline each **prepositional phrase**. Circle the **prepositions.**

17. The children knocking at the front door live around the corner.

18. Mary hid the letter beneath the books on the top shelf.

You're on your way!

Skill Drill Grammar Answers

Page 2
1. Shirley; Saturday; . 2. The; Ms. Alberts; . 3. Did; Dr. Swift; ? 4. How; ! 5. Do; Neil Armstrong; ? 6. Jackie; I; New York; May; . 7. Will; Father; Mr. Jackson; ? 8. Did; Pepper; ? 9. Our; ! 10. We; New Year's Day;. 11. My; Judge W. Heinz; German; . 12. Having; . 13. What; ! 14. Professor Jenkins; . 15. Cousin Billie; I; Chinese; J. J.'s; .

Page 3
1. Larry, 2. Barbara,; Bertha, 3. Mr. R. B.; wasn't; June 10, 1998, 4. Karen,; San Francisco, CA, 5. Monica's; pool, 6. comedy, mystery, 7. batter's 8. Yes,; August 14, 9. B. J.; hasn't 10. Prof.; Diaz,; Dr. 11. lettuce, tomatoes, 12. When, Mary, 13. Ms.; Wilton, Minnesota, 14. Well,; I'm; Norway, Iowa, 15. Tammy,; bread,; milk,

Page 4
Indirect quotations are numbers 2, 3, 5, 7, 8, 9, and 13. Remainder are direct quotations.

Page 5
1. "Carry Me Back to Old Virginny" 2. "Jingle Bells" 3. "The Start of the Monsoon" 4. The Victory at Ribbon Pass 5. "Learning to Fish" 6. A Famous Race Horse 7. Red Badge of Courage 8. "Mice" 9. "Race Against the Clock" 10. "Alexander's Ragtime Band" 11. The Call of the Wild 12. "She'll Be Comin' 'Round the Mountain" 13. "Valse Triste" 14. A Scout's Handbook

Page 6
Teacher's judgment.

Page 7
Teacher's judgment.

Page 8
1. it's 2. I'm 3. that's 4. we're 5. what's 6. we've 7. he's 8. you've 9. you're 10. don't 11. it'll 12. won't 13. hadn't 14. haven't 15. they'll 16. where's 17. shouldn't 18. we'll 19. weren't 20. aren't 21. I've 22. you'll 23. let's 24. can't 25. he'll 26. didn't 27. she'll 28. doesn't 29. they've 30. they're 31. she's 32. hasn't 33. there's 34. isn't 35. I'll 36. who's 37. wasn't 38. wouldn't

Page 9
1. Henry; Jess; town 2. mouse; rodent 3. Joey; shoes; school 4. Math; subject 5. Bertha; Tim; floors; windows 6. meal; hamburgers; potatoes 7. Grandpa; car; driveway 8. Ellen; hair; 9. father; city 10. Barbara; Connie; piano 11. Mother; dollars; blouse 12. Rose; Grandma; bouquet; daisies; birthday 13. Otto; races 14. John; Marta; newspapers; bundles. 15. Kisha; Statue of Liberty 16. Carol; Las Vegas; weekend 17. Michelle; Jonathan; house; Bogardus Avenue 18. children; bus; noises 19. Jess; crate; apples 20. farmers; grapes; Coachella Valley

Page 10
1. game; badminton 2. Badminton; game; world 3. Badminton; game; countries; Thailand; Indonesia; Malaysia 4. people; countries; England; Denmark; Sweden; game 5. man; Rudy Hortono; Indonesia; championship 6. Mr. Hortono; streets; statues; babies 7. Chris Kinard; United States; champion 8. scholarship; U.C.L.A.; trips; countries; England; Canada 9. Badminton; sport 10. rackets; players; shuttlecocks; birds; net 11. Badminton; tennis; ways 12. player 13. players; United States; trophies 14. players; money 15. players; United States; game; tennis

Page 11
1. candies 2. knives 3. pianos 4. axes 5. potatoes 6. armies 7. copies 8. teeth 9. heroes 10. halves 11. friends 12. children 13. journeys 14. solos 15. calves 16. shelves 17. duties 18. groceries 19. enemies 20. cities 21. cupfuls 22. loaves 23. babies 24. feet 25. valleys 26. taxes 27. tomatoes 28. lives

Page 12
1. spider's 2. Mother's 3. dogs' 4. children's 5. Fluffy's 6. Mr. Samuel's 7. calves' 8. sister's 9. dog's, Mother's 10. Ladies' 11. girls'; boys' 12. Karen's 13. boy's 14. Jim's 15. Today's 16. America's 17. bee's; Jenny's 18. Mike's; cake's

Page 13
1. Donna's; Skipper; Meyer Ave.; Palm Park; . 2. Have; Mother; Aunt Vivian; ? 3. Look; ! 4. My; I; Dr. Benson's; May 2,1998. 5. Did; Mr. G. Daniels; Phoenix, Arizona; Tuesday; ? 6. Gail, Jerry,; I;. 7. Kelly,; ;. 8. The; Irish; St. Patrick's Day;. 9. "I...party," Aaron 10. Each; "My Favorite Day of the Year." 11. Henry; A Sea Otter in My Backyard 12. shouldn't 13. he'll 14. they're 15. that's 16. Benny-proper; friend-common; Westwood Theater-proper; movie-common 17. mice 18. taxes 19. trays 20. wharves 21. pianos 22. radios 23. berries 24. potatoes

Page 14
Teacher's judgment.

Page 15
Numbers 1, 2, 5, 7, 10, 11,15, 16, 18, 21, 22, 25, 28, 29, 31, 32, 35, 36, 37, 39, 41, 45, and 46 are nouns. The rest are pronouns.

Page 16
Numbers 1, 3, 6, 9, 11, and 14 are linking verbs. Numbers 2, 8, 15, and 16 are helping verbs. Numbers 4, 5, 7, 10, 12, and 13 are verbs.

Page 17
1. had fallen 2. have eaten 3. were swimming 4. did see 5. should have done 6. were written 7-18. Teacher's judgment.

Page 18
Complete subjects are: 1. Sandra 2. Many monkeys 3. Paul 4. My father 5. The rain 6. My cousins 7. six inches of snow 8. We 9. The small child 10. Aunt Susan 11. The little boy with curly hair 12. The driver of the small red car 13. Mother 14. The sleepy children 15. The large dog with the brown spots 16. Our tiny canary 17. David 18. The loud noise

Page 19
1. report 2. cheesecake 3. Jack 4. Mother 5. home run 6. purse 7. package 8. children 9. blouse 10. children 11. pie 12. me 13. books 14. sandwiches 15. Edna 16. truck 17. Maryann 18. water

Page 20
1. everyone 2. Nicholas 3. me 4. friends 5. us 6. Dad 7. Miss McGregor 8. Maria 9. Mrs. Lawson 10. Shirley 11. relatives 12. Amy 13. Ralph 14. boys 15. Grandma Olga 16. us 17. Mom 18. nephews

Page 21
Teacher's judgment.

Page 22
Write an for numbers 2, 9,12,14, 23, 24 25, 32, 33, 37, 39, 42, 43, 45, 46, 53, 58, and 59. Write a for the remaining numbers.

Page 23
1. laid or lay 2. laid 3. laid 4. lie 5. lying 6. lain 7-13. Teacher's judgment.

Page 24
1. risen 2. raising 3. raised 4. rose 5. raise 6. rose 7. rising 8. risen 9-15. Teacher's judgment.

Page 25
1. pronoun 2. noun 3. verb 4. verb 5. noun 6. pronoun 7. had thrown 8. has read 9. could have done 10. did complete 11. Natalie and I-subject 12. Joey-subject 13. Richard and Mom-subject 14. book-D.O. 15. Melissa-I.O.; card-D.O. 16. me-D.O. 17. a 18. lay 19. raising 20. risen 21. lying

Page 26
1. Aegean Sea 2. Riverside County; U.S. Highway 10 3. Senate 4. Far East 5. Boy Scouts of America 6. University of Michigan; Stanford University 7. Department of Agriculture 8. American Airlines 9. Fountain Road 10. Spanish Club 11. West Virginia 12. Whittwood Theater 13. Los Angeles; California 14. Veterans of Foreign Wars 15. North America; Asia

Page 27
1. Reader's Digest 2. Everybody's Favorite Ghost Stories 3. "Hamlet" 4. Charlie and the Chocolate Factory 5. "While Strolling Thru' the Park One Day" 6. Florence Nightingale 7. "Moon River" 8. Newsweek 9. Time 10. "When Johnny Comes Marching Home" 11. "A Christmas Carol" 12. National Geographic 13. "I Walked Through the Forest" 14. "Ode to Autumn"

Page 28
Numbers 1, 4, 6, 8, 9, 11, and 12 are subjects. The remaining numbers are objects.

Page 29
1. me 2. He 3. we 4. She; her 5. They; us 6. them 7. him 8. I; them 9. She; I 10. me 11. him 12. her 13-16. Teacher's judgment

Page 30
1. Whose; your 2. It's; your 3. There's; your 4. Who's 5. You're 6. theirs 7. its 8. It's 9-16. Teacher's judgment.

Page 31
Teacher's judgment.

Page 32
1. feet 2. due; week 3. eight; flowers 4. sent; aunt 5. two; fair 6. hall; right 7. scent; rose 8. toe; rode 9. sew; new 10. see; principal 11. stationery; write 12. colonel 13. straight; piece; wood 14. threw; pair 15. hole; pail 16. cereal 17. made; loan 18. Their; no

Page 33
Teacher's judgment.

Page 34
1. Every-adj.; child 2. tired-adj.; hikers 3. talkative-adj.; group 4. old-adj.; barn 5. frail-adj.; bird 6. almost-adj.; everyone 7. several-adj.; oranges; fruit-adj.; stand 8. crisp, crunchy-adj.; cereal 9. rough, rugged-adj.; cowboy 10. buttered - adj.; toast 11. bright - adj.; sunshine 12. tall, dark, handsome-adj.; man; that-adj.; bank 13. silly-adj.; joke 14. terrified-adj.; puppy 15. dangerous-adj.; curve 16. seven-adj.; dollars; 17. difficult, spelling-adj.; words 18. tattered, torn-adj.; curtains

Page 35
Teacher's judgment.

Page 36
1. slept; here-adv. 2. ran; fastest-adv. 3. did leave; seven-adv. 4. shouted; loudly-adv. 5. proudly-adv.; showed 6. played; quietly-adv. 7. flew open; suddenly-adv. 8. swims; easily – adv. 9. unusually – adv.; good 10. takes; Tuesday, Thursday – adv. 11. landed; safely – adv. 12. working; hard – adv. 13. can ride; almost – adv. 14. talked; nonstop – adv. 15. predicted; accurately – adv. 16. made; recently – adv. 17. seldom - adv.; has; 18. boldly – adv.; raised

Page 37
1. My; South; May 2. We; Texas; Continental Airlines 3. Gilbert; Willow Creek 4. Joseph; Rutgers University 5. Little Women 6. "My Favorite Friend and I." 7. Sports Illustrated 8. Family Circle 9. subject; 10. object 11. subject 12. object 13. scent; flowers 14. pear; two 15. adj. 16. adv. 17. adj. 18. adj. 19. adv.

Skill Drill Grammar Answers

Page 38
1. The 40th president of the United States of America; president 2. The tired kitten; kitten 3. Nancy; Nancy 4. That tall boy; boy 5. The billowing black smoke; smoke 6. Pretty pink streamers; streamers 7. The cool night air; air 8. The large spider plant; plant 9. Jackie; Jackie 10. Rusty; Rusty 11. A guided tour of the Los Angeles County Museum; tour 12. Lori; Lori 13. Our school band; band 14. Two brown buttons; buttons 15. Our public library; library 16. Many people; people

Page 39
1. jumped onto the rock near the water's edge; jumped 2. cheered for our favorite team; cheered 3. dropped one more quarter into the machine; dropped 4. examined the jacket carefully; examined 5. is a frisky animal; is 6. asked for volunteers; asked 7. ate all the seeds; ate 8. are in the same race; are 9. cannot make their own seeds; cannot make 10. purchased a new saw and hammer; purchased 11. threw the newspaper in the trash can; threw 12. has moved to Lincoln, Kentucky; has moved 13. will help cook dinner tonight; will help cook 14. flew to Arizona on Wednesday; flew 15. carried her blue umbrella to school; carried 16. are learning a new magic trick; are learning

Page 40
1. and 2. and 3. and 4. and 5. but 6. or 7. and 8. for 9. but 10. and 11. or 12. but 13. and 14. and 15-18. Teacher's judgment

Page 41
(Two part answers will be compound subject; conjunction.) 1. blouses, skirt; and 2. peanuts, raisins; and 3. Mother, Aunt Rita; and 4. Terry, Patty; or 5. books, magazines; and 6. Clifton, I; and 7. Coffee, tea, milk; and 8. dog, cat, boy; and 9. Bobby, family; and 10. Swimming, jogging; and 11. Milk, butter, eggs; and 12. doctor, nurse; or 13. friend, I; and 14. Tomatoes, carrots, cucumbers; and 15-16. Teacher's judgment.

Page 42
(Two-part answers will be compound predicate; conjunction.) 1. went, opened; and 2. cut, watered; and 3. tripped, hurt; and 4. typed, studied; and 5. will bake, buy; or 6. stopped, ordered; and 7. may trim, plant; or 8. purchased, filled; and 9. dove, swam; and 10. baked, cut, served; and 11. erased, wrote; and 12. washed, waxed; and 13. sliced, toasted, buttered; and 14. will sing, dance; and 15-16. Teacher's judgment.

Page 43
Teacher's Judgment.

Page 44
1. at 2. by 3. on 4. in 5. toward 6. with 7. on account of 8. under 9. after 10. between 11. among 12. above 13. to 14. from 15. in 16. over 17. due to 18. behind

Page 45
Write Time for numbers 5, 7,12,15,16, and 18. Write Cause for numbers 3, 8, and 13. Write Direction for numbers 2, 9,14, and 17. Write Position for numbers 1, 4, 6, 10, and 11.

Page 46
1. to Salt Lake City; to 2. While we watched the movie; while; to buy popcorn; to 3. in my science class; in 4. within the hour; within 5. at Hollywood and Vine; at 6. in the pink dress; in; in the choir; in 7. among the trees; among 8. of milk; of; from Lucy; from 9. after school; after 10. behind the department store; behind 11. of spaghetti; of; from my hands; from 12. to the music; to; of the new band; of 13. at Grandma's house; at 14. Due to Washington's birthday; Due to 15. up the street; up 16. near the seashore; near

Page 47
1-14. Teacher's judgment. 15. subject 16. object

Page 48
1. his 2. who 3. who 4. his 5. his 6. that 7. her 8. that 9. that 10. who 11. who 12. his 13. which 14. who

Page 49
1. Look out! 2. Alas! 3. none 4. Slow down! 5. For goodness sake! 6. Hurrah! 7. Aha! 8. Look! 9. none 10. No way! 11. Please! 12. Bah! 13. Cheers! 14. All right! 15. none 16. Watch out! 17. Stop it! 18. Oh my gosh!

Page 50
1. exclamatory; ! 2. interrogative; ? 3. declarative; . 4. imperative; . 5. imperative; . or exclamatory; ! 6. exclamatory; ! 7. interrogative; ? 8. imperative; . 9. declarative;. 10. declarative; . 11-14. Teacher's judgment.

Page 51
1. boy – subj., ran – pred. 2. Peter – subj., will help trim – pred. 3. Jackie, I – subj., enrolled – pred., and – conj. 4. Roberta – subj., sang, played – pred., and – conj.; 5. Roses, carnations, daisies – subj., are – pred., and – conj. 6. Kathy – subj., may buy, make – pred., or – conj. 7. Allen – subj., jogged, swam, played – pred., and – conj. 8. Due to bad weather – due to 9. on the counter – on 10. at the library – at 11. She, me 12. that; 13. his 14. who 15. interrogative – ? 16. imperative – . 17. declarative – . 18. exclamatory – !

Page 52
1. One; Mrs. J. Adams; Christmas 2. Someday; I; Steven 3. This; Mrs. Adams; Highlights 4. She; Norman Rockwell: The Illustrator Everyone Knows 5. When; Mrs. Adams 6. Norman Rockwell 7. His; Miss Smith; Norman 8. During; Norman; Wednesday; Friday 9. Norman; Chase School of Art; New York 10. When; Norman; National Academy School 11. Edward Cave; Boys' Life; Norman 12. Mr. Rockwell; Saturday Evening Post 13. He; Tom Sawyer; Huckleberry Finn; Louisa May Alcott: America's Best Loved Writer 14. Every; Norman Rockwell; Boy Scout 15. Mr. Rockwell's; Arlington; Vermont 16. I; Mrs. Adams; Steven 17. My; Thanksgiving Day; Loretta 18. The; Irish; French; Chinese

Page 53
1. Mrs. L.; April 13, 1981. 2. Denise,; ?; 3. Avenue, Culver City, California. 4. out! 5. Paul,; Michael,; . 6. Yes,; . 7. Hasn't; ? 8. Ian's; Yolanda's; . 9. "By the Seaside"; . 10. Sesame Street; ? 11. "Becky – here,"; . 12. said,; "Dr. – principal." 13. June 18, 1995,; Melbourne,; Australia,; . 14. dog's; . 15. girl's; or! 16. "Will you,"; Mother,; "be – nine?" 17. We're; Pat's; house,; . 18. "Irene's – Avenue,"; . 19. ! 20. T.; won't; . 21. Aha! 22. "No, Randy, I'll – September 19,"; .

Page 54
1. father's 2. one; week 3. an; a 4. lying 5. raising 6. Men's; sale 7. An; meet 8. to; buy; an; two 9. Lay 10. child's 11. Cindy's; blew 12. lay; rise 13. who's 14. you're 15. there's 16. couldn't 17. I'm 18. we'll 19. large; small 20. light; dark 21. energetic; tired 22. simple; difficult

Page 55
Write interrogative for numbers 1, 6, and 9. Write exclamatory for numbers 2, 3, and 10. Write declarative for numbers 4, 7, and 8. Write imperative for number 5. 11-17. Teacher's judgment.

Page 56
1. Sylvia, Hubbard's Department Store – proper 2. test, test – common; Thursday – proper 3. Grant Avenue, Lincoln Boulevard – proper; house – common 4. will speak 5. are coming 6. slept 7. Kathy – IO; rose – DO 8. Susan – IO; vacation – DO 9. Bread – DO 10. computer – DO 11. Christine – IO; basket – DO 12. at the creek; at 13. in his shoes; in 14. Due to the strike; Due to 15. under the bridge; under 16. around the house; around; over the fence; over 17. Alas! 18. Hold it!

Page 57
1. Norman Rockwell – subj.; painted – pred. 2. Melissa – subj.; lives – pred. 3. Leslie – subj.; is preparing – pred. 4. man – subj.; is directing – pred. 5. John, Sam, I – subj.; wrote – pred.; and – conj. 6. Mary, Nanette – subj.; will play – pred.; or – conj. 7. I – subj.; read, wrote – pred.; and – conj. 8. California, Texas – subj.; are – pred.; and – conj. 9. for 10. but 11. or 12. and 13. and; and 14. but 15-18. Teacher's judgment.

Page 58
1. My; I; our; her 2. We; them; their 3. They; it; your; it; mine 4. subject 5. object 6. subject 7. object 8. she 9. him 10. We 11. Who's 12. his 13. that 14. her 15. us 16. that; him 17. me 18. They; us; them 19. I 20. theirs 21. that

Page 59
1. carefully – adv. 2. bright, early, one – adj. 3. soft, luxurious – adj. 4. lightly – adv.; crispy – adj. 5. moody – adj.; selfishly – adv. 6. white, lace – adj. 7. slowly – adv. 8. dark, mysterious – adj. 9. tired – adj.; yesterday – adv. 10. quietly – adv.; cozy – adj. 11. ant 12. penny 13. read 14. house 15. rain 16. flowers 17. handkerchief 18. shattered 19. moved 20. neighbor

Page 60
1. R.J. Smith; Meadowlark Avenue; . 2. My; friend's; Annabell; March 3,; . 3. "Nonsense!; I'm; it!"; George; . 4. When; Dr. Kenneth Johnson; Thanksgiving Day; "America the Beautiful"; . 5. Larry,; Jimmy,; Brad; Manchester,; New Hampshire,; Monday,; Wednesday,; Friday; . 6. Elizabeth's; East; Santa Clara Native American; . 7. Did; Nora; Irene; Girl Scouts of America; January; ? 8. While; France; Aunt Rachel; French; . 9. "Gil, – me?"; Mrs. Lee; . 10. Teddy's; I Love You, Dear Dragon; . 11. Andy,; said,; "Jerry; I; Yellowstone National Park; Memorial Day weekend." 12. Oh,; don't; Inside Sports; ? 13. fragment 14. declarative 15. imperative 16. run-on 17. exclamatory 18. interrogative

Page 61
1. An; through 2. he; who 3. she; raising 4. rise 5. two; pairs 6. that 7. He; rose; he; lying 8. us; her 9. I; them 10. We; see; our; their 11. Whose; laying 12. They; me 13-24. Teacher's judgment.

Page 62
1. preposition 2. noun 3. adjective 4. noun 5. pronoun 6. verb 7. adverb 8. interjection 9. preposition 10. conjunction 11. pronoun 12. adjective 13. Janet – IO; secret – DO 14. package – DO 15. I – subj.; her – obj. 16. we – subj. 17. at the front door; at; around the corner; around 18. beneath the books; beneath; on the top shelf; on